To Liz ...... Bill
Hof
Love ... (Patsy)

Meet Me Halfway

A collection of writing
from the
Bennettsbridge and Derry Writers

CELEBRATION OF FRIENDSHIP
WOMEN WRITERS
DERRY-BENNETTSBRIDGE 1994

First published in November 1997 by
Guildhall Press, 41 Great James Street,
L'Derry, Northern Ireland BT48 7DF
Tel: (01504) 364413 Fax: (01504) 372949
E-mail: gpress@compuserve.com

ISBN 0 946451 45 1

Guildhall Press receives support from the Training & Employment Agency under the Action
for Community Employment scheme.

Cover design Bennettsbridge/Derry Writers and individual artists
Typeset and designed by Joe Mc Allister
Printed by Coleraine Printing Company

Special thanks to Manus Martin (T&EA), and Derry City Council's Recreation and Leisure
Department for generous Community Services Grant Aid.

ACKNOWLEDGEMENTS

The Derry/Bennettsbridge Writers would like to thank the following who have assisted in making the exchange programme possible and in the publication of this anthology:

Co-operation North

Derry City Council

Northern Ireland Voluntary Trust

Northern Ireland Workers' Educational Association

All the facilitators and workshop leaders who
have assisted the group over the past three years.

All those people in Bennettsbridge, Thomastown
and Kilkenny who have so generously supported
the group in the past.

FOREWORD

I doubt that any reader will be able to resist the sparkle, the energy and the unpredictability of this book. I certainly wasn't. Very often, in reading an anthology, one page will tell you something about what to expect on the next. But this isn't the case here. These are wonderfully different, wonderfully definite pieces of work. It would be invidious to mention names – and unnecessary, because readers will discover for themselves – but the quick shifts from a patchwork quilt, to a seaman's death, to a photograph bringing both pain and memory – these are the register of the emotional vivacity and the rich cultural life which the writings here accurately record. Here are the objects and events of the lives of women, in and between generations, enacting themselves in remembrance, anger, happiness.

This in itself would be enough to make this anthology a special event. The poems are often beautiful and heart-wrenching. Some of the prose is funny, downright and biting. In other words, everything is here for enjoyable and memorable reading: for closing the door, putting on a kettle, shutting out the rain and finding somewhere comfortable to read and laugh or be pierced by some equivalent feeling.

But there is another dimension to this book that takes it beyond even this central value. This book is the outcome of meetings between writers in two different groups: in Bennettsbridge and Derry. To note that members of one group write openly about the effects of conflict in daily life, while their fellow writers in the other group approach that dailyness in a more sheltered society would, I think, be to miss the point. What makes all these writings fresh and convincing is that they are the record of private feelings, private lives. Those lives and those feelings happen at all times, in all places, under all conditions. What is remarkable and poignant is that in a society where the circumstances of these lives can divide people from each other, these writers have found a way to share the deepest life of all: the imaginative one. They have done so in the most resolute and generous way, and the evidence is here for all to see. This is a wonderfully humane, interesting and engaging book. It has a beautiful and instructive title. As one of its first readers, I congratulate the writers involved for their work, and for their communal grace. And I recommend it warmly to the many others who I know will enjoy it as much as I have.

Eavan Boland

INTRODUCTION

This joint publication is tangible proof that distance is no obstacle to positive co-operation. The North/South groups involved here have come together in the depths of Winter and the height of Summer to share a variety of experiences. They talk, think, write, tell stories. They laugh, cry, sing, argue and philosophise. They also benefit gastronomically from an exchange of cuisine and culinary skills, and artistically from a display of arts and crafts.

Since meeting they have begun to refute all historical bias and misrepresentation. They have learned to listen to their own voices and the voices of others.

They began to express their own thoughts and write them down together and, in doing so, caught a glimpse of the lives of a whole generation of Derry women amid conflict and violence, while their counterparts in the South looked on, sheltered by the security of relative peace.

The origins of the joint group go back to 1989. Members of a Maynooth based Social Studies group in Bennettsbridge, County Kilkenny, set the scene for what was to become the Bennettsbridge Writers.

Meanwhile, in the Derry Women's Centre, under the auspices of the WEA, women were coming together to form a creative writing group. About this time a member of the Bennettsbridge group, who was also involved with Co-operation North, made a phone call to the Northern women to negotiate the possibility of a cross-border exchange between the two. To quote Chris Head, there was a resounding "Yes, yes, yes!" from a province which was fogged in by "No, no, no!"

The first meeting was in Derry in October 1993 and from then on women, from two or more different traditions, set out in a spirit of optimism, on a journey of understanding, through the common ground of creativity. They had chosen a new way.

In all about four exchange meetings have taken place. In 1996, eight years after the Bennettsbridge/Maynooth Studies Group had progressed to writing, they were back in Maynooth again. This time the Derry/Bennettsbridge group met to plan their own strategy for this publication. When investigating the particular venue, one of the negotiating parties suggested "Meet me half way," and so, with these simple words, was born a basic philosophy for this group of women and a symbolic title for the joint publication which they now proudly present.

CONTENTS

Gathering to Write

Ancient Ways

Carousels

Conflict

Peace

Personal Postcards

Final Act

Gathering to Write

Gathering to Write

Between the sea and mountains
I notice small stones
snugly embedded in dark sand
similar, not the same.

Are these stones of the
mountain or of the sea?
I draw a circle
feeling the moist sand ripple around my heel
encompassing a random number.

Now I have a circle containing stones
yet my awareness is of people
similar, not the same.

I am entering a circle to write,
this circle opens
to embrace strangers from the north
to share
to sense
to define
our lives, our histories;

Circle closes.

Daphne Hunt

Maynooth College

Beautiful.
Golden candles gleam and glow,
Lofty frescoes pull eyes upwards
Where some prayers could never go.

Imposing.
Solid walls that will not bend,
Testament to man's achievement,
Built and kept by poverty's stipend.

Controlling.
Womankind feel alien here.
Dear God protect our sons
When life here makes it hard to bear.

Immovable.
Progress can't break through these walls.
Isolated and alone
Young boys can't hear mothers' calls.

Ina Cantrell

St Eugene's Cathedral

The cathedral on the skyline
looks cold and austere
a stern reminder of darker days
when my soul lived in limbo

The church gave me no succour then
and when the organ played
the rhythm only touched my feet
Heart cold stone.

Now I dance with joy
the cathedral
no longer stares me down
nor church, nor man can invade my spirit
My heart and soul are alive to a rhythm
that surrounds me

Janie Richardson

Bonding

On a crisp October evening
I headed for Badger's Bar;
An apprehensive woman
Who thought she'd gone too far,

To meet a group of strangers
Who had just arrived in town
For a Creative Writing weekend
And have a look around

Old Derry's walls, the Guildhall
The museum and the bog
And to meet with Derry women
Who'd help to raise the fog,

That blinded them from seeing
Just what was going on
In that other part of Ireland
So troubled and war torn.

With introductions all around
My fears began to fade,
For these Kilkenny women
A base for friendship laid.

With their warmth and love endearing
Us to each and every heart.
They cared for what was happening
In this land, so torn apart.

They asked us down to Bennettsbridge,
Their village on the Nore,
A greensward under orange skies,
Peace oozed from every pore.

A sturdy oak we planted there
Upon the village green,
Beside the rock of friendship
That sealed the bond between

Women writers, North and South
Different, yet the same
No matter what the future holds
Our friendship will remain.

Margo McCartney

The Long Week-End
Bennettsbridge/Derry Writers
1994 & 1995

Memories shelved
then taken down and
rattled; legends shared
unravel the mystery that is
our future

A patchwork quilt
stitched with precision
now adorns our wall
each square a reminder
of individual pain,

Death strides this week-end
with poetry, food and friendship;
conflict fuses with courage
and our patchwork history is
woven into our
fragmented lives.

Janie Richardson

Pilgrimage South

To Bennettsbridge by invitation
We asked Betsy for a ride,
Without a moments hesitation
She invited us inside.

Off we took from dear old Derry
Mary T was at the wheel,
Margo and Phyllis in the back seat
I played navigator/reel.*

But it's a long, long trail awinding
On the road to Bennettsbridge
When the signs just aren't for finding
And you can't see o'er the ridge.

When you think you're heading southward
And you batter on with pride,
Then suddenly there's the sign 'ATHLONE'
And you shrivel up inside.

Mullingar, oh Mullingar
We've passed you twice within the hour,
We loved your banners, bars and wines,
But where oh where are your bloody signs?

As Betsy's driver wheezes onwards
With a fag in either hand,
And darkness creeps ever forwards
Is Kilkenny never-never land?

Half a day is spent in travelling,
Twelve long hours with little rest,
And as tempers start unravelling
Betsy's passengers are past their best.

Was it worth it? Never doubt it,
We're with friends we love so dear,
Bennettsbridge is just like heaven
We'll be back again next year...

As we leave, departing sadly,
Headed back to stress and strain,
One thing stays with us forever -
Forget the driving — take the train!

*reel = idiot

Ina Cantrell

Salmon Steak
(Exchange visit, Maynooth 1996)

Pinked flesh clung to the frying pan
soaked up juice of sage parsley
and country butter

Our palates ran with anticipation
as we obeyed the child instinct in us
we bore the intolerable weight
of a weekend stolen from hearth
and crock filled sinks

We beggared pennies stretching coinage
into golden nuggets to buy memento's
of the football pitch Midlands

No mount broke horizons as tortoise shell outlines
hemstitched grey vistas, holding up
the steeple to glorify the heavens

Colcannon versus Champ
yellowed and embedded with onion
the humble potato levelled us all

A gourmet meal cooked by women
who showed their queenly grace
despite their fragile auras

Courage wrapped up in that culinary feat
onion and garlic did not shed a tear
and that salmon steak never tasted better

Elma Khareghani

Breakthrough

Finally pushed to the limit
she lifts up her head and is heard

'You argue, you fuss
you debate and discuss
'til I feel I must shout
please shut up and listen
take time out to hear me
you haven't a clue
what it's all about'

In the silence that follows she tells us
the problem from her point of view
"We're sorry...
Forgive us...
We didn't mean to offend
We just weren't thinking of you."

Eileen Lynch

Medicine Women

We came into a room
alight with candles
disguised as women
washing the air
with scents of friendships' femaleness;
We shared our gifts
describing them in crayon
and felt-tip pen,
colourful paper circles
forged holes of light in an old schoolhouse floor

we know this place
we sense this space

Embraced in a wheel of female arms
We danced the dust off sleeping spirits;
These fields, our face,
soft and chiselled with living,
These tools, our hands,
suppled and crippled with making,
These rivers, our heart,
flooded and dried with loving,
This space, our essence,
tugged for renewal in the ancient way.

Chris Head

Ancient Ways

The Dispossessed

The spectral figure moves across the Island,
Where mountains and valleys
Touch bogland and craggy slopes meet
Bays of golden sand and crashing sea.
The keening wind echoes and re-echoes
The grief of lost generations.

Here cluster roofless ruins:
Mute monuments to ruthless famine.
Did these walls once ring with laughter,
With the sound of céilídh, music and song,
To be silenced by death?

The shadow follows the coastline north.
Here isolated relics stand
Of evictions: forced emigration.
The keening of lost generations
Echoes and re-echoes across the barren land

Now a change comes over
this ancient land:
New houses, television antennae;
Alas, few sounds of laughter.
The young have gone.

The cries of lost generations
Echo and re-echo
From glen and mountain top.
Must this land
Always remain
Island of the dispossessed?

Eilis Heaney

The Visit
New Year's Eve 1995

I

Grey skies domed Benone Strand
afraid to warm us with a ray of sunshine

A brisk walk down the beach
over sand sculpted by gale force winds
grasses leaned from its biting force

Though bodies well wrapped
it found every chink and vent
drew saline drop from eyes
half closed against the minus factor

Crash of waves on the crescent shore
driftwood and shell trawled from the deep
punctuate the vagrant water line

Suddenly our alien steps faltered
a sign proclaimed "Firing Range"
map reminders rivet us to this place
defiled by the Ministry of Defence

We dared go forward for a heart beat
willing to breach a law of trespass

We trespassed and turned our broad backs
kicking a discarded can to vent our anger

II

On this grey December day in Portstewart
we admired the pastels that lay on her table
charged with light
that sucked us into its Newgrange brilliance
making nonsense of the melting snowman
gazing houseward with his charcoal eyes

A woollen scarf did not save him
it lay sodden on the famished grass
a dog played with his eyes, buried them deep
between dormant bush, bulb and root

Clink of glass and sláinte in varied accents
filtered through a veil screening
an inner chamber with its solstice light
ancestral bones rattled in a ceremonial bowl
chiselled glyphics on kerbstones
did not make us understand that race

We turned away and cried over melting snow

III

Giant's Causeway for once sheltered from the wind
gigantic steps reach out to the North Pole
as Neptune learned to play Gaelic football
forgot to kick over the sandbars
losing the game to Davy Jones
who bribed the team
with Coral Sea Pearls and Spanish Gold

Stones did not speak that Eve night
as we ascended to the Grianan of Aileach in robust
procession
and chanted our way along narrow ramparts

A lone candle glowed in the earthy cauldron
warriors stood fast, Celtic shields lowered
ready to do battle at our behest

We shocked them into cold silence
with our peaceful wish for the province
and the light was blown out
by a teethed wind harvesting the unwary
but the reaper was ousted by the chime of a new day

Elma Khareghani

Famine Stricken

I stagger from the pit
Where my babies lie
February winds sear
My watery eyes
Heavy lids droop
Wretchedness engulfs me
Bleak landscape
Speaks no hope
Stench of death
Smothers me
My head swirls
My legs crumble
Face in the gravel
Despair consumes me.

Somewhere in the distance
A horse neighs
Carriage wheels rumble
In my delirium
The landlord's manor
Stretches out of reach
Or, as vision fails,
Is it the workhouse
Looms before me.

Rose Kelly

The Orange Man

I once knew a man
who said he was my father
this is true
I often see him
when I look in the mirror.

He used Brylcreem
wore brick-coloured overalls
and rarely came home
before my bedtime.

His wealth consisted of three ha'pence
there was no limit
to the things he could do
with these coins.

My mother said
he was the only person
she knew who could
peel an orange
in his pocket.

Helen Crimin

Nettles

There are no snakes in Ireland
But along the country lanes and hedgerows
Where the wild raspberry grows
Lurks something just as deadly.

Quietly it lies in wait
Among the bluebells and the gooseberries
Then, just as the naked hand
Reaches to pick the berry
The silent nettle weaves gently in the wind
To caress and sting
A sting more deadly than the bee

And the anticipated sweet taste of the berry
Is all in vain
And once more you realise
The prize is not worth the pain.

Ina Cantrell

Grianan of Aileach
(New Year's Eve 1995)

Rapt on Winter's embrace
    we slid and skipped through the snow
until we reached the ancient fort.
    Our candles, cradled in jars
competed against an ice cold wind
    that tried to penetrate our hearts.

Warriors stormed through crumbling walls
    intent on conquering this hallowed force
and phantom cries of war
    screamed from gaping wounds
as they surged toward us.

The moon paled through snow cloud;
    In poignant silhouette we clasped hands
encircled the fort made our secret wishes
    then cried out loud to the aggressor

"Sacrifice your rage   Sheath your sword!"

Janie Richardson

The Young Musician's Song
(For John McDade — born into a troubled Ulster)

The only rose without thorns is
the wild rose. Sing Minstrel, sing
of gentle lives, of beauty and
of love. Sing of the Celtic rose
that smells so sweet
yet breaks the heart.

Cast out iron girders.
Water the arid desert
with your sweet song
and let fall mantles of
tears, like myrrh to moss.
Sing until snow-bound mind and
flesh surge, warm again.
Chip stone into form
most meaningful with
your melody.

Let sparkle sad souls
on the saddle of your song.
Play on Minstrel.
An overture to
glad to-morrows.

Daphne Kirkpatrick

Good Friday

On Good Friday morning
She climbed the hill
The little old woman
From the little old mill.
Bent with a bundle of wood
On her back
She wore on her shoulders
A ragged old sack.
She stumbled along
Through briar and moss
I couldn't but think
Of Christ and His cross.
She turned and faced me
As I passed by
She stared me boldly
Eye to eye.
She was bent and wrinkled
Old and spent
Spoke not a word
As on she went.
I felt it strange
On this blessed day
That such as she
Should pass my way.
It seemed that somewhere
Back in time
Her dilemma
Was *my* crime.
Did I hammer nail and thorn
On that first Good Friday morn?

Rose Kelly

Big Tommy
(A tribute to my father)

A fair mountain of quiescent calm,
Large work-worn hands gently soothed
The pains of childhood.

Oddly limpid eyes of green and blue
Gazed compassion, when flowing tears
Stained our faces.

A coherent wisdom, gained by years of
Sailing life's oceans, lucidly
Awakened us.

Compelling yarns of schooners and coasters
And foreign lands
Enthralled us.

Guinness and Woodbine contented,
Strains of 'La Cucaracha' or 'O'Donnell Abu'
Amused us.

Dying... a penniless seaman,
We, not realising then
Our inheritance.

Margo McCartney

Blessed are the Meek

Hawthorn smoulders, filling the wood-
stove
with deformed claw-twigs.
Like spider crabs they sigh
bleeding their sap.
Smoke scent swirls on the down-draught,
Berries still cling, mulled and darkened
by their late autumn condition.

In that other garden.
the Garden of Remembrance,
the severed branch
that was my father's life
is rendered by its autumn condition
to primitive embers
and ritual cleansing.

Daphne Kirkpatrick

The Gift

The gift on the mantelpiece throbbed with a tribal beat
girthed the equator and the steeple in the background
collapsed with the heat of the fire emblazoned
on that flinty spear

My dreams are full of an arrow head
given to me by Ina, my friend

Our blood lines passed through from the same eve
she of the long night haunts ghostly mansions
her crown scented with heather and musk
she drifts through a haze of grace and beauty
her blue eyes reflect well water ready to drink
her body vagrant to her wish sinks into the warmth
raucous strains filter through walls
discordant to the veins hungry for oblivion
and still we sang a world's repertoire
until the spreading dawn fingered the corners
through the open windows

I choose to think it did not penetrate living flesh
only of that wisdom and firedance flash
in the orangelight that ornated the doeskin tent
radiating from its lodgepoles holding up the sky

Elma Khareghani

The Co-Existence Tree

Who dares to share a branch with me
In this my monkey-puzzle tree?

See how it spreads, so thick and high,
Maze-like and dark against the sky.

The deep green branches cold and bare,
No gilded fruit or berry there.

Instead, the faces that I see
Will light this barren Christmas tree.

Every image stark and bright,
My Chinese lanterns of the night.

Here come the soldiers, run like hell,
The sight of them sets off the warning bell.

The pompous, the pious, the tired politicians,
Whatever they do, it's the same old conditions.

And now see the young men, the pride of the town,
They sing as they sigh, as they die as they clown.

Then everywhere children, swaying and swinging,
Their faces are legion and gladness they're bringing.

How many, how few?
How false, how true?

The ghosts of the past continue to climb,
To sit beside them, to turn back time.

Daphne Kirkpatrick

Famine Woman

I dragged myself down to the shore
not to listen to the gulls
or hear the rush of wind

sand between toes

damp black shawl
hugs my small frame

this winter harsh unrelenting
no currachs dare venture forth
some sold to buy grain or seed

the hunger is on us

I turn the stones for anything

a shore raped of its seaweed
all living things

no energy to dig
nails cracked and broken
to dig for worms

Whisht, I hear a strange sound
it's a seal caught in the rocks
I lift a stone and bring it crashing down
its puppy eyes pleading
I beg forgiveness my need is great
those hungry ones are waiting waiting

she looks at me
I see wisdom and love
she turns her silky head

I bring the stone down again
the light in her eyes dies
a tear rolls down her jowl
to join the Atlantic

with renewed strength
I get my knife
chop at the warm flesh
wrap it in my shawl

I bury the rest for later
scan the horizon
there's no-one there
satisfied I bring my precious gift home

Elma Khareghani

From the Casket to the Women of 2045

Will you squeal
as only children can
when treasures are opened?
And will you feel
our journey
as you finger our maps?
Are you free to be
who you are?
Is your choice an informed one?
Are you in charge
of your spirit, your health?
Are your faces open and clear?
your feet sure in their step?
Are your eyes steady with knowing?
Do your ideas flourish?
Are you at yourselves?
Have you found your true colours?
Are you able to make
the world work for you?
Do you read between the lines?
Is that still necessary
or did honesty find a hold?
Is the air clean?
the water fresh?
Are the borders gone
the tribes well met?
When you open me
will you smell our breath?

Chris Head

(the casket maker)

Carousels

Mistaken Identity

I kissed a stranger on the cheek that night
She stood on the corner in Thomastown
looking quite lost
I thought she was one of our guests from Derry
I rushed   I gushed
I welcomed her profusely
Silently she gazed at me
then picked up her travel bag
and walked toward the waiting bus

Janie Richardson

A Gentle Personality

"I really am a very mild natured person," the little woman at the bus stop said to her friend. "It was just that I really lost the rag that night I cut the legs off his trousers."

She was small, thin, sharp featured. She talked quickly and loudly. She continued her story: "I was really mad with him that night. He was going to go out, no matter what. So, while he was in the bath, I just got the scissors and went to the wardrobe and cut this much," indicating a length of about eight inches, "off the legs of his trousers. Then I put them back in the wardrobe and I went down and sat at the television. And you never heard anything like the roars of him when he found out. He sat and sulked all evening. But I was driven to it. Normally I'm the mildest of women, it would take something really bad to get me going."

She did not say where this recalcitrant husband had been intending to go, why she objected, or whether he did not possess another pair of trousers that he could have worn.

"And then there was the other night he had a mate in, and they sat and talked all evening. Then, when his mate got up to go, they stood and talked for ages in the hall. And then they talked for ages again, standing in the doorway. And would you believe it, they weren't finished even then. What did they do if they didn't stand talking out on the street! Well, I had had enough by this time, and I got a bucket of water and went up to the bedroom window and poured it out on the two of them. And you know, that's not like me at all, as I have such a gentle personality. But there comes a time when you can take no more. If I hadn't thrown the water on them they'd have talked out there forever."

She went on to tell more, many more, tales of how she, a mild and gentle person, had been aggravated beyond endurance. Her companion, a seemingly quiet and mild woman, smiled and nodded agreement from time to time.

She told about the woman in her local grocery, who had sold her some vegetables that were not fresh; and when she took them home and weighed them, they were under the weight she had asked for. So, she called the shopkeeper a thieving old ratbag, not that she'd talk like that normally, you know, but it really got to her the way people in shops took advantage of her good nature and served her any old rubbish.

She told about the time the police called about the NO WAITING stands she had taken from the street. But she had needed them for the bit of street outside her front door. People kept parking on her bit of street, with the result that often they had no space for their own car. So she had lifted four NO WAITING tripod stands from the main road and had firmly planted them along their bit of street. Then, when they wanted to park their own car, all they had to do was lift the signs and put them inside the front door.

Well, she couldn't believe it the day the police called and told her it was illegal, and not only was it illegal but she could be charged with stealing the tripods. And she just let them know that if they were doing their job as they should there wouldn't be any parking problem outside the front door. And, of course, the reason the police gave her this hassle, and the reason that people parked there anyway, all boiled down to the fact that she was so gentle by nature that she would never stand up for herself, and people could sense that, and they would take advantage of her.

She was so absorbed in her monologue that she did not, at first, notice the bus approaching. Then, suddenly, as she became aware of the queue starting to move, she remarked to her quiet companion, "Here's the bus now, you need to mind your place in the queue, people would think nothing of pushing onto the bus in front of you."

And the little, mild-natured, gentle woman firmly elbowed her way onto the bus, darting intimidating glances at anyone who might try to push past her.

Sive Haughey

Life's Merry-go-round

I wrote a list
of things to do
a poem for Derry
a letter to you.
Bread for the birds
fuel for my fire
phone 'what's his name?'
about my tyre.
Go to the bank
plead my case
check 'The Times'
for the 3 o'clock race.
Shoes to the cobbler
along to the shop
struggle home laden
no time to drop.
The library has sent
another card
in trouble again
it's never hard.
Pay the milkman
buy the bread
A new tax disc already?
keep the head.
It never ends
this merry-go-round
Oh! mustn't forget
the dog from the pound
"To sleep, to sleep, perchance...

Helen Crimin

Hullo Mr Hen

It happened every quarter... as regular as the full moon. Terror struck our otherwise quiet street. It was as if the residents were awaiting the wrath of God to descend upon them. Every man, woman and child, froze at the mention of his name. He was coming to collect his dues. Well, not his dues really, but the stipends for the upkeep of the clergy of the parish. He was appointed by the powers that be, to go to each Catholic home in the area and gather as much money as the working-class could part with, and God help anyone who was not forthcoming.

Everyone called him 'Jimmy the Hen', but nobody was quite sure why. Some said he had only three toes on each foot, others said it was because he was always picking the last morsel from the pockets of the poor. I, myself, thought it was because of his beaky nose and his staring eyes, which never seemed to blink.

Jimmy's day job was usher at the local picture house. There was no carry-on at the Saturday matinees. If you went to the toilet more than once during the film, or got over excited when Tom Mix, Gene Autry or the Lone Ranger were chasing the baddies (well you couldn't help but shout and jump up and down in your seat, just to let them know you were on their side and you were riding with them all the way) Jimmy's torch would come down on your head with such a force that it wasn't only the stars on the screen you were seeing. There was no child-line in those days with Esther Rantzen at the end of it. You just had to take your oil.

My mother, God rest her soul, not a woman to be easily intimidated, was a nervous wreck the week before Jimmy was expected. A ten shilling note was placed beneath the china dog on the mantelpiece days before the impending visit. Sometimes that ten shillings meant the difference between steak and peas, followed by custard and jelly, for our Sunday dinner or a pot of soup with a couple of spuds thrown in. If my mother had to make a choice then soup it was. Jimmy had to get his money. What's more, it had to be there for him the moment he knocked on the door. He didn't like to be kept waiting. If he had to rap a second time he became very annoyed and would ask: "Are you deaf?"

I've known families who didn't have the money and rather than face him would take themselves off for the day, maybe walk to the top of Sheriff's Mountain. Some spent their Sunday afternoons huddled under the kitchen table. These sort of actions put Jimmy in bad form, (not that anyone had ever seen him any other way). So, to register his annoyance, he crossed their name in red ink. That way the clergy knew at a glance exactly who the defaulters were.

Jimmy's reign of terror ended when the Catholic Church, in its wisdom, decided to become ecumenical. No more Latin masses and instead of door to door collections we were given little coloured envelopes like our Protestant neighbours took to Christ Church on a Sunday. Now some say that Protestants are God's chosen people and I could well believe it, owing to the fact... they never had to face 'Jimmy the Hen'.

Margo McCartney

Train Spotter

Old man at the station
Watches the trains go by,
Day after day.
He comes and goes
Waiting for someone?
Nobody knows.

Brown felt hat
On bent old head
He waits for comrades
Long since dead
Father mother
Brother friend
He'll wait for them
To the very end.

And while he waits
Maybe he'll yearn
For someone
Who will not return.

But look!
I see a gleam
In his eye
He just likes watching
Trains go by.

Rose Kelly

Invitation

I declare I'm over fifty
short and fat those are the facts
hunting down valleys
and the long roads of this island
but you're never satisfied
with that

You want to get into my head
forage for food inside
you've found me out
brain cells dead
not fit for dog food

I'm a catholic uncatholic
married to a state
that changed with the seasons
buying and selling souls

You've found me out I'm an atheist
who believes in life after death
what a waste you contemplate
harvesting breaded brains
you're welcome to come dine

What side will claim me
if the cease-fire no longer holds
I don't give a damn, just
scatter the ashes here and there
as long as it's on this isle
you're all invited to the knees up after

Elma Khareghani

The Missing Teddy

Teddy is missing, where has he gone?
And he just recovering from surgery.
Poor little lad was it homesick he was
And has he made his way back to Derry?

He came down here after the All-Ireland
In nineteen ninety-three
When Derry were football champions
He was presented by Mary T.

We'll send an identikit picture to Crimeline
In the hope he may be found
Was he teddy-napped, I wonder
Oh, if I could catch the hound.

We'll get our local correspondent
At the Kilkenny People to make a plea
Whoever took our Teddy
Send him back immediately.

Oh, please return our Teddy
He was our mascot don't you see
And we're offering a reward
To have him brought back safely.

I think about poor Teddy
Who's tucking him in at night?
With the Derry crest upon his tummy
And his coat of red and white.

We've searched around for paw prints
We've written to Pat Kenny
Will the person who has taken him
Please return him to Kilkenny.

We'd give him a great welcome
If he came back home
And we'd place him on the lotto box
Never more to roam.

Phil Kennedy

Forgive us our trespasses

I accompanied her to mass
In the grey stone church
Her silver hair
Blue rinsed... religiously
She sat beside her friend, as usual
As they whispered and nattered together.

The mohair scarf caught my eye
It was new
The rainbow colours of
Soft wool beckoned.

During mass the scarf
Slithered down onto the floor.
To the chant of "Our Father..."
I watched and planned.
Eventually, we left the building
The two women still chattering.

I found an excuse to go back
Looked around; the church was empty.
Swiftly I hid the scarf under my coat
And slunk away
Put it into a drawer at home
Never to see the light of day.

Anne Buckley

The Mighty Oak

I am an oak tree. I stand here in a green patch beside the road. Nearby is a large stone which reads "Celebration of Friendship – Bennettsbridge/Derry Women 1994." I am not here very long as I replaced the original oak tree that was planted in or around the same spot. From what I can gather, the first tree was planted at the same time the large stone was unveiled but, unfortunately, it didn't live very long. I am told it was well looked after, watered and fed, but perhaps it was a bit on the delicate side. I hope I'm made of stronger stuff. I enjoy being here.

I have some tree companions so I am not lonely. Anyway, I see lots of people passing by every day so it keeps me occupied. The postman comes by every morning on his way to deliver the letters. School children walk by, sometimes discussing a forthcoming hurling match or some other happening in the school. The milk man, delivery vans, buses and trucks are a common sight.

One day recently a lady came by wheeling a sort of motor bike. I heard someone say it was a 'moped'. Every so often the woman tried to start the engine. I believe it is called 'kick starting'. After a few attempts she succeeded and I could hear her singing something about 'Belonging to Glasgow' as she chugged out of sight. A man came with another sort of engine recently and cut the grass. One of my older companions told me it was a lawn mower. The green looked very tidy when all the grass was cut and the cuttings taken away.

The weather is lovely now, nice and sunny; but it can be very cold. I don't mind the rain as it is good for me and helps me to grow but the wind frightens me. If it is too strong it could uproot me from the ground and I might share the same fate as my predecessor. I hope the birds will build their nests in my branches and that one day I'll be known as 'The Mighty Oak'.

Phil Kennedy

Last Orders

When I die
Don't bury me
Burn me -
In sawdust and cedar
Not sapele and satin,
'Cause sawdust burns better
And cedar smells sweet;
So with that combination
I'll go up a treat.

Don't dress me in glad-rags
Just T-shirt and jeans,
That's all I've liked wearing
And God knows where I'm going
So practical clothes are the scene.

Pack all my oils,
My travelling spoils
My postcards and letters
From you kids and my betters;
My mousy's, my pendants,
My bumbag – my beaker
That says Mums are sweeter
And anything else
I might need on the way.

Don't scatter my ashes into the sea
Or some dark, dreary place;
That's not for me;
But on top of a hill
So I'll catch a fresh breeze
And drift on to the places
I've packed up to see.

Don't pine for my presence
Just remember the laughs
That we've all had together
In years gone past.

Then I can be happy
To get on with my tours
While you lot
Are just planning for yours.

Diana Guy

Conflict

Crossing the Divide

Today I walked over the bridge
      flanked by walls
I crossed the divide between South and North
      listened to a hostile tune

Today I walked over the bridge
      listened to the fear created by fear
to the anger rising from that fear
      to the prejudice that fought to be free

Tomorrow   when I cross the bridge
      I will climb the wall of indifference
and listen to a quieter voice

Janie Richardson

The Killer

I looked into his eyes and saw nothing.
I gazed on his face
And saw the trained killer
Without human emotion.

Just an instrument
Of the State.
I felt not hatred
But realisation.

He had taken the life of my beloved son
Yet I could not hate him
Just the regime that gave
This automaton the right to kill.

Eilis Heaney

War was alive in our house

No memories of the North as a child
No television until the early '70s
No room in my head for any other tragedy
But to survive my own.

The eldest of ten children
Working in the factory
My wages handed to mother.

After sewing children's clothes
Lunchtime consisted of
Two rounds of bread and
Tea begged from another's flask.

Half-an-hour's walk home
Feet wet from wearing
A stranger's old shoes
To be greeted by a bleak empty grate.

Father did not provide

Mother sat taking the barrage of anger
From wet hungry children.

Constant physical and verbal violence
Never knowing in what mood
Father would arrive home.
Watching my mother's face
I knew what to expect of the day.

Kathleen Brennan

Despair

My emotions, a barren shore line
Distorted by the touch of salt water seas.
Like an abandoned sand castle
My heart crumbled
My dreams washed away
By reality
Swept out to sea
Diluted
Overwhelmed
Destroyed
I drowned in salt water

Linda Morgan

Derry on Sunday Morning
(17 October 1993)

The
'Diamond' deserted
the bustle of Saturday
hushed. Isolation -- Desolation
I walked headlong into
the Mall studded
only with
soldiers

and
almost tripped over
a camouflaged, doe-eyed
boy, strategically positioned at
a corner, kneeling, green
beret tilted, gun
at the
ready

Children
with toys of war
protecting Patrick Mayhew
in a church
down the
road

Children
like mine, led a
charmed life, until the
tragedy of Derry
overtook
them

Janie Richardson

Fear

You know
That the back door is locked
That the iron is switched off.

Why do you go back?

You know
That you have your purse,
Your keys

Why do you go back?

You know
That you don't really need that shopping bag,
That your gloves are in the car,
That you don't really need to sweep the hearth before you go.

Why do you go back?

You know
That it's only a few yards
From the door to the car

Why do you hold back?

You were in time
Before the ritual of fear.

Now you're late.

Sive Haughey

In Whose Name?

Your purpose is done
Your mission was none
That we ever wanted

Go find a new way
Or just stay at bay
Your bullets and bombs
Will never hold sway

You shout and you tease
You say bombing will cease
Then you shatter your promise
But we still want peace

Try as you might
I pity your plight
You will never succeed
You don't have the right

Eileen Lynch

Womb Talk

Encased in a tomb of someone else's making
Bombarded by heavy thudding drumbeats;
Hated, undesired, resented and rejected,
I lie and await my fate.

But be warned, my Mother. If I go
I'll take much of you with me
For we are one and the same;
You should have considered your own future
Before you ever gave me mine.

Baby: Conceive me.
Mother: I mustn't.

Baby: Love me.
Mother: I can't.

Mother: Be gone from me!
Baby: I won't

Mother: Don't grow on me!
Baby: I will.

Mother: Don't die on me.
Baby: I have.

Diana Guy

Green Jacket

I passed him every day on my way to school. I was unaware of his presence. Well, that's not quite true, I was aware of men, but not of him. He was stationed in a large, newly erected, stone and cement bunker that had been constructed on waste ground adjacent to my granny's house. I had to pass both on my way to school. I was told by my parents to keep to the right side of the street. He stayed imprisoned on the left, incarcerated for fear of death by sniper bullet. Sometimes, when I passed, I could hear them call across the road; I would put my eyes downward and inspect the ground I was covering in my rush to pass by. I didn't look up. I pretended I didn't hear their calls. I would increase the speed of my walk and escape their gaze by turning the corner and entering the school gates.

It was a ritual throughout my early days at primary that, in the afternoon, my mother would make her way to my granny's house where she would wait for my release from school. On cold winter days my cousins and I, all girls, would drink hot tea and eat large pieces of freshly made bread smothered in strawberry or raspberry jam. We would all sit around the large square table enjoying our feast, then hands and faces would be washed with a soapy flannel. On many occasions I was sat up on the draining board of the sink and my mother would lament the fact that I seemed to attract more dirt than my female counterparts. Knees washed and dirty socks turned inside out to give the illusion of lady-like demure, we were ready to walk home.

We had recently acquired a new addition to the family. It was at times like this I felt the new baby was an asset, as I slung my school bag onto the goods tray of her blue pram. I was always instructed to hold tightly onto the steel handle of the pram and help push the baby home. Usually, on these walks home, my mother and I would discuss my day, or rather I talked and she listened. All the while she would clasp her hand around mine entwined about the plastic ribbed covered handle of the pram, while the baby slept. A memory to the years we had walked, just the two of us, hand in hand, home.

Since granda's death we called to granny's with even more regularity. In the evenings my father would check the windows and doors, bring in the coal for the morning fire and leave granny secure for the long lonely night ahead. Our car had just turned the corner when you stepped out and put up your hand indicating that we stop. In the dark of the evening I didn't look at your face. I just knew from the cut of your uniform and gun that you were a British soldier. I didn't know any British soldiers.

You indicated to my father to pull the car inside the concrete construction. Once secured, he was asked to get out and proceeded to open the bonnet and boot; the usual procedure. Then you tapped lightly on the window of the passenger side and opened the car door. My mother, with the sleeping baby in her arms, looked up. You put your gun down and lowered yourself onto your hunkers, eye level with my mother and I in the car. "She must be two month's old now," he looked lovingly at our sleeping baby. "I have a boy." I looked at his helmeted head; I saw a beautiful face. As a child I could not understand beauty, was it his eyes, his mouth? I didn't know. All I knew was that to me he was beautiful, because he was soft and caring.

He reached deep inside his flap jacket and, from beneath the security of his body armour, he produced photographs of a baby. He looked lovingly at the boy and told us he wished he had been able to hold him. He hadn't seen him yet; he hadn't been home; he only had these photos. In the dim light he held the photos aloft for us to look at. Suddenly he said "I'm so afraid I'll never hold him. I'm afraid I'll die before I can go home." My mother held our baby closer and then patted the hand that held the baby photos. "Please God you will be all right." I wanted to put my arms about him and hug him to me. Fear kept me rigid in my seat. "I've watched you." He told how he had watched my mother every day. He knew our movements each day, at what hour. He knew from the way she looked that he could talk to her, but he couldn't just stop her in the street, he didn't want to put her at risk, he knew we were all afraid. He apologised for his outburst, but he just needed someone to talk to, he had no-one. He was a commanding officer, he had to show strength to his men, but all he wanted was to see his baby and the wife he loved. It was two weeks until he got home. My mother promised she would pray for him.

My father opened his door and climbed into the car. "Thank you ma'am." He used his thumb and forefinger to tip his tin helmet slightly forward, a man's gesture towards a lady, a thank you. He stepped aside and gently closed the car door, aware of our sleeping baby. We were signalled to proceed. The car slowly edged forward and we moved out of his life. I looked back, he was standing looking at us depart.

For weeks after that night we quietly prayed and, sometimes, when passing the sangar, I looked secretively towards the peep holes and wondered was he there inside, watching us. No soldiers were killed during that two weeks and I felt relief.

Linda Morgan

Division

Could I understand
the pain and fear

Of the mother whose son
is beaten up

Or the wife whose husband
doesn't come home

Of the Canadian wife who
lives in isolation because
her husband is a constable

How could I
living in the South
understand
their pain, their fear.

Eileen Lynch

Mothers

One, her only daughter lost
A ruthless assassination.
Another, three sons killed.
Yet another, a beloved son
Coldly murdered.
Still it goes on
This litany of endurance.

From this core of stoicism
Passed on for generations
In the face of constant oppression
Must come a free land
Without fear
A land of equality and peace.

Eilis Heaney

Taboo

We never came this way, or if we had it had been on a very odd occasion. My father's brother lived at this end of town, he didn't visit. I had been playing in the back seat of the car with my older brother, rolling and sliding about on the dark green ribbed leather seat. We would sometimes pull the arm rest down from its hidden position midway along the back of the seat and use it as a vantage point on which we would perch to have a better view, or as a dividing line neither would cross during a squabble or row. Then, we would place our childish limbs on its cool leather and secure as much of the arm rest as possible, two arms slapping and pushing against one another to gain the greater part of the territory. The car had stopped in the cold frosty evening. My father made no movement but sat imprisoned behind the wheel. We both looked ahead, my brother and I, past the forms of our parents, through the newly formed raindrops on the windscreen, to the ill lit street ahead.

"Daddy, daddy, look at those men!" I raised my young plump hand, forefinger outstretched, to guide all our eyes to a point where they were already fixed. No-one spoke. The feud erupting in the back seat between my brother and myself was instantly forgotten in the grip of fear that had captured us. I slid forward in my seat, desperate for the comfort and reassurance that had prevailed all my childhood years. I slid both hands about my mother's neck and rested my face in her hair, closing my eyes, trying to block out the scene outside the car, but the atmosphere overwhelmed me. I was uncomfortable and afraid. A fear that seemed to seep through my very being, for I sensed my parents were also afraid.

I could smell my mother's scent and feel the soft curls of hair press against my face. She was warm, but trembling. My arms at full stretch were not yet long enough to encompass her and I held the index finger that I had pointed to the scene outside securely between clenched fist, to join my hands. It was a strain, but I held tight, as my mother gently patted my weakening grip. I could feel the soft skin of her throat against my hands. She was swallowing silently.

Suddenly, the door at my father's side of the car opened. Cold night air invaded the car. A balaclava'd face gave orders to switch the engine off. He noticed my brother and I in the back of the car and said in a low tone directly to my mother: "Won't be long." My mother nodded appreciatively as she did to people in the street indicating good morning, good afternoon, a pleasant recognition; but we didn't know this dark clad stranger and there was nothing pleasant about this situation.

My eyes had become accustomed to the lack of light and we all watched the guns pass along the human chain, man to man. Each face clad in black balaclavas. We sat watching, knowing that we had stumbled across a secret. A deadly, dangerous, secret.

I watched as glittering metal passed along from secure hand to secure hand, making its way along the chain until it disappeared behind a high wall.

Then the chain splintered into fragments, like broken pieces of glass or pottery. The men scattered in different directions and disappeared into the night. The car resounded with the sounds of three heavy thuds to the roof. We were left alone in the street. It was still raining. The car windows were completely misted over and water ran down the insides of the glass from our heavy, hot, breath.

Instinctively we all knew the three thuds on the roof meant we could leave. It was over. We were free to go. My father started the engine and turned on the lights. The street was empty. We drove home silently. We never travelled that way again, nor have we ever discussed the incident. We kept it as much a secret from each other as everyone else. I wonder do they still remember, as I do.

Linda Morgan

The trouble with peace is...

Can I take those faltering steps
Make the journey across the bridge
Peer over the top?

Can I bring my gifts of common sense
Empathy and positive regard?
Tear down the barriers
Break down the walls?

But where will I hide
With my fears
My prejudices
My secret admiration for the bearded Sinn Féin man
My dislike of the fat, smug Unionist politician

My pain?

Anne McLoughlin

When men of Power...

When men of power
Elected by the people

Sit at smooth mahogany tables
Paid for by the people

To determine the future
Of the people

It's worth remembering...
Land has no party politics

And grass will grow
Without the people

Ina Cantrell

Peace

Solitude at Runkerry

On Runkerry's sweeping crescent strand
Even the gulls have taken flight.
Pearlsoft mist bathes rocks and sand
In clear translucent shimmering light,
Paints marram grass and sandy dunes
With a gentle brush in pastel hues.

A marled foaming restless sea
Rushes towards the rocky shore,
Throws up flotsam and loose debris,
Then melts away with a hissing roar:
And only the boom of the surf intrudes
Upon Runkerry's solitude.

Diana Guy

Derry

This city looks so peaceful at night.
Amber lights reflect
On the dark deep river Foyle
That cuts through politics and people
On its way to the greater ocean
Sharing itself with all
Equally.

Ina Cantrell

Derry in Perspective

Soft shadows play on warmed pavements
St Columb's bell tolls
as worshippers stroll by daffodil and tulip
up to its imposing door

Across in the Women's Centre
women ask delicate questions
that touch their lives
live on the edge

They share the tapestry of their co-existence
conflict left on the landing
to shiver in the cold winds of late spring

Elma Khareghani

Maiden City

Those who pray for peace
Surrounded
By parents pushing prejudice
Misguided myopics
Bequeathing
Death and destruction to
A generation
Too young to understand.

Ina Cantrell

Derry Derry

Derry Derry
quite contrary
how does your river flow
Past fields and valleys
streets and alleys
forever in the know.

It knows those who
are sleeping
It knows who is awake
Those who plant
and those who reap
who gives and
those who take.

She dances in glittering sequins
beneath a summer sun
In her winter greys
she skulks and sways
and watches all that's done.

In the dead of night
she passes
amid a thousand eyes
intent on busy business
with the foolish
and the wise.

Oh, Derry bright
in pale moonlight
or warm in the summer sun
I wish you peace
I wish you love
may your Foyle
forever run.

Helen Crimin

A Peace Process

A woman,
standing in her backyard at night
felt lucky,
she could still see
between hard lines of brick and slate,
the soft mass of hills
steadfast in their skirts of feral sea
and only an hour away
if ever she needed them.

In the street today I passed
some men, oblivious to the potential
of language,
no and never and no
surrender, and no compromise
themselves to a standstill.

A woman,
propped in her doorway at night
felt the ease
of warm July air
charming her mind with old playmates,
Lucid, Luminous, Lupine,
so clear, the divine, her full-bodied wines
and always there,
if ever she needed them.

In the park today I watched
a child, look at the world upside down
then crash, and
squeal and laugh and frown,
gathering air in tiny hands,
setting it free without sound

A woman,
sitting in her kitchen at night
watched the shadows
of leaves rustling

from the only tree in the alley,
recharging the white walls
yellowed by smoking and cooking,
but only at night
when she most needed them.

In the alley today I heard
a mother, dragging the heart and shell
of her life
backwards and forwards from
task to task, heaving and sighing
herself to oblivion.

A woman,
lying in her bed at night
kissed the dark
and held it tight,
the line on which she'd hung her life
fell into bits, and died.
She buried them well
and smiled.

Chris Head

Peace is a right

The trouble with peace is
it's not really meant
to be taken too literally
until war is all spent
between different factions
parties and race
and the bombs and the guns
are extinct from the face
of this glorious earth
we call Mother – in trust
of an end to all wars
and a world that is just.

Peace is a right
not easy to find
it's elusive, nervous,
timid, kind.
It is that state of grace
toward which we all strive
that eternal hope
which keeps us alive

Janie Richardson

A New Beginning – 1994

Peace be with you
We said
St Eugene's Cathedral Derry
Sunday morning
We clasped hands.
In the grounds outside
Daffodils waved in the light April drizzle
Beside blood red tulips
Sharp reminder
Of lives lost
In twenty-five years
Of troubled times
Hands clasped A new beginning
Peace be with you
Derry

Joan Cleere

Personal Postcards

Postcard from Bali

The bird flew out of a tree
into the light of the moon
watched by a cyclopic eye.

Like that flying bird,
bird of freedom,
you migrated,
escaped the dark undergrowth,
dived like a moth towards bright light.

Light of deceptive beauty,
cold, unwelcoming, infertile
you went to find your soul
you lost your way.

Mary-Margaret Kelly

Photo

I found the photograph
Hidden among papers, bills and notes
A ghost
Frightened
Enthralled
I fingered it lightly
Remembered
You
Us
I held it in trembling hands
Wanted to throw it from me
Longed to hold it to my heart
Longed to tear it limb from limb
I stopped
Angry at myself   at you
Carefully, I put it back
Closed the lid
And walked away

Linda Morgan

Lost

Have you seen her lately?
You could find her
Buried beneath a pile of ironing
Standing by a sink stacked high with dishes
Pushed aside to make room for school books
Behind a steering wheel
En route to a parent/teacher meeting.

Is that her?
Leafing through household bills
Organising meals
Soothing troubled feelings
Smothered in the depths of earthly problems
Weighed down with responsibilities

Have you seen her lately?
Please look carefully
You could find the woman
Who got lost somewhere along the road
Between children, home and community
You can set her free
To walk in the country
And listen to the singing of the birds
To sit beside the river
And watch the water flow past
To search for adventure,
To live again.

Joan Cleere

Letting Go

I have stolen,
for my children
coal,
when I needed to,
and for the thrill of it.

I have told lies
when honesty
threatened
to humiliate me,
to keep myself right.

I have laughed
too loud, for too long
at the wrong things,
a splendid display
of redness about the roots.

I have made declarations of love
to too many, too quickly,
too scared to say no,
afraid that my life would be halved.

I have cried lakes
in the hope
that someone
would leap in and save me,
a performance not to be missed.

I have agreed
too often
without thinking,
wagging and smiling,
gathering feathers into my nest.

I have cast
my eye inward
and found,
a simpler way, a new journey
every day, letting go, letting go.

Chris Head

Hiding

I'm not afraid
I tell myself
I won't be afraid anymore
I'll be brave
I tell myself
I'll break down that ebony door

What ebony door
is that my child
What ebony door do you mean?
The ebony door
I stand behind
with a soul that can't be seen

But your soul
belongs to God my child
your soul belongs to Him
and He can see
through hard black doors
and He can see your sin

Don't frighten me
with talk of sin
don't frighten me, I say
if He has knowledge
of my soul
what need of doors this day

What need of doors
indeed my child
What need of doors at all
for it's not a door
that hides your soul
but a protective self-made wall

Don't touch my wall
I need this wall
to build it took me years

I can't expose
my soft white flesh
my blood my sweat my tears

I've changed my mind
I am afraid
I need that ebony door
I need my wood and stones intact
They
may not like my core.

Helen Crimin

"And that's too much..."

He sits on a bright day
In darkness.
The light his eye sees
His mind does not comprehend.
Unmoved, he watches
Other people's lives
And they watch his.

He knows no peace,
His heart is full of terror,
Images, wild and free
Invade his mind.
Swirling mists impede
Each faltering step.
Walls are soft as velvet
Rivers gleam.

This oblivion
Is all there is for him.
No joy, no hope, no pain
Like other folk.
Because, if anything matters
Everything matters
And that's too much.

Eileen Monaghan

My Derry Friend

I met Cathy when I worked in the Deaf School in Dublin. I was asked to do substitute for a teacher who was sick. I was brought into the classroom and introduced. One of the girls in the class started to cry. She wanted her own teacher back. I was nineteen years old and feeling very nervous and this grief-stricken-sixteen-year old did nothing for my confidence.

I 'lived-in' at the school and had a cubicle in one of the dormitories. There were about six or eight beds in the dormitory. My cubicle had partitions which were about six-feet high and beside the door there was a window, so that I could check on the girls at any time. The reason the partition did not reach the ceiling was so that I, being the only person without a hearing impediment, could raise the alarm if anything should go wrong during the night.

Cathy very quickly overcame her grief at the loss of her teacher and we were soon very good friends.

Cathy was from Derry. She was only partially deaf and could hear if there was no background noise. Her speech was excellent when compared to the totally deaf girls and I could understand her very well. She had a younger sister in the school also. Her name was Sheila and she was totally deaf.

I remember being amazed when she introduced me to her mother's boyfriend, who drove a red sports car. Parents being divorced, or even separated, was a new thing to me at that time.

Within a few weeks of the first day that I met Cathy she had, I later realised, developed a crush on me. She did not sleep in the dormitory which I supervised, but when I went to my cubicle I would find a note from her on my bed which she had thrown over the partition. She would tell me in her note how much she liked/loved me. Sometimes I would find a 'treat' such as a can of coke or a bar of chocolate outside my door.

I went home to spend a weekend with my parents about twice a term. One Sunday, when I returned from a weekend at home, I was met by a babble of teenage girls gesticulating and articulating that Cathy was in some kind of trouble. When I had calmed them down I finally discovered that Cathy's mother had come for her on the Saturday to take her home. She would not be coming back to the school. The girls told me that Cathy had been extremely upset and had left a letter for me.

I found the letter on my bed. Cathy had obviously been distraught when she wrote it. She had no prior notice of leaving school and wanted to stay. It was only then that I realised that she had left school permanently, but I never discovered the reason why. The following day I got a letter in the post. I wrote back immediately. I received a letter from Cathy every day for at least two weeks and then they gradually reduced to three, two and finally one a week.

I invited Cathy to my home in Carrick-on-Suir during the following Summer holidays. She accepted the invitation. Her mother's boyfriend drove her down. I have no recollection of his name. She stayed with us for a week and my young brother and sister really enjoyed her visit. She didn't want to go home at the end of the holiday and her letters were more distraught than ever for sometime afterwards.

My memory of a time span is not good, but I know we corresponded for a number of years. I remember getting a letter from her when I was on holiday in Mitchelstown. She told me about the people for whom she baby-sat and said she didn't want to baby-sit for them any more because the father used to come back to the house when she was there on her own and wanted to have sex with her.

I was totally shocked and extremely upset for her. I was still a virgin myself at that time and couldn't conceive of that type of abuse. Even though I was around twenty-one years old at this time I felt totally inadequate to help her in her predicament. I didn't have any adult myself that I could ask for advice, but I wrote back to her and asked her to tell her mother about this abuse, stressing the fact that it should not be happening and that the man was in the wrong. I also told her that if she felt she could not tell her mother that she should tell a priest or some other person 'in charge'. I was really a very naive twenty-one year old.

One day, a year or two later, I received a letter which was postmarked 'Derry' but which was not from Cathy. It was from a friend of Cathy's mother and it was to tell me that Cathy was very sick and in hospital. There was a telephone number on the letter and I rang from work in Cork that day. I spoke to the friend who had written to me and she told me that Cathy was dead. She had been taken into hospital with a brain tumour and had died before anything could be done. She was twenty-one years old at the time.

I wrote to Cathy's mum expressing sympathy and my own grief at Cathy's death but that was the last contact I ever had with Cathy and her family.

More than anything else, when I think of Cathy, I realise now how ill-equipped I was to deal with this young deaf girl who came from a culture totally different to mine. I never knew there were differences between Catholics and Protestants, or if I did it was purely academic. I didn't know that all Catholics did not go to Mass on Sundays or that many Catholics had sex before they were married or that Catholic parents separated and even divorced, or that a young Catholic girl could be abused sexually by an adult, or that any young girl could die from a brain tumour when she was only twenty-one years old. I wish I had known these things and many more when I knew Cathy Smith who was a young, deaf, Catholic girl from Derry, who boarded in a school for the deaf in Dublin in the mid-sixties.

Eileen Lynch

Stealth

Something's missing
Something's adrift
Sky descends
And will not lift
All my thoughts
Merge into one
For something's missing
Something's gone
Endless search
Pursuit or quest
In crowd or solitude
Work and rest
For all my query
There's no riposte
For something's missing
Something's lost
It eludes, evades me
Day by day
This something that's missing
Slipped away

Rose Kelly

Extract from "Tread Softly"

But I think thirty seven's a lovely age, for anything. And it's the sort of age you can get away with for about ten years if you're lucky. And even if you're not, no-one really expects a woman to reveal her age; they all add on five years after you've told them.

Thirty seven is magic! It's that marvellous period in your life when you know everything. You know if your child is faking a tummyache to get off school; you know a bargain when you see one; you can tell the time roughly without a watch; you know two and two can sometimes make five and, of course, you are sexually liberated at last, especially since you got your tubal ligation!

I think every woman should have one. The joy of being able to have uninhibited sex during those ten wonderful days in the month when you look good, feel good, and by golly you are good! Days when you can go ten rounds with your husband without it being a knockout in the third. Days when you leave him dazed and asking weakly, who was that masked woman? Days which had been no goes, unless of course you were trying. Now all yours for the enjoyment of; trying or not.

Mind you, I never had to try very hard. I read somewhere that it usually takes one hundred and thirty ejaculations for a woman to get pregnant. I only needed one! Three babies in thirty three months told me that. But that kind of break-neck production only brings trouble. You don't love me any more; you think more of those kids than you do of me; and the biggie, will you ever really want me again? The kindest answer at this stage is, look, fuck off and find a nice eighteen year old nymphomaniac, and leave me in peace! Just keep sending the maintenance money.

But you don't give it, and he wouldn't do it anyway. So you struggle on with the bottles, nappies, strained food, strained relationship, until one day you wave the last off to the secondary, and your troubles aren't little ones anymore, they're much bigger. But you're thirty-seven and you can cope with anything.

Of course Deirdre of the Sorrows had the right idea. Get out while the going's good. When you reach the peak of your relationship have him murdered, then kill yourself. Seven glorious, passionate, untrying years she had, and not a stretch mark to show for it. How lucky can you get? I suppose it would be too much to expect fey, beautiful women to procreate. Perhaps that's left to mother earth's – like me.

It would have been interesting to have seen the issue of such a great pair of lovers as Deirdre and Naoise though. Maybe it would have been something like the baby that Wonderwoman and Superman are reputed to have produced; you know, the one that nobody knows the sex of, because they can't catch it.

Christ! How did I get on to all this? Isn't it amazing what goes on inside your head? My husband never ceases to be amazed at what goes on inside mine. In fact he says if a lot more went on outside my head we'd all be much better off. He's probably right.

Myra Dryden

She leaves flowers for the altar

I remember
Your blonde hair
Gold rings, varnished nails
Well spoken voice

I remember
Our meeting in the launderette
When I brought in the weekly wash
Your kindness
Your attention

I remember
Going to your home
Scrubbing, cleaning
Eating biscuits whilst
Polishing your son's shoes
Black ingrained on palms
And fingers

I remember
Sitting, surrounded by mahogany
Laden with silver and fine
Bone china my small face
Distorted in gleaming silver spoons

I remember
My childish fantasy as I caught
The scent of flowers in the room
Daffodils hugged your garden path
Watched me enter your door after two
And leave before six
Coppers in clenched fist

Kathleen Brennan

She Threw Nothing Out

She threw nothing out,
Kept every artifact
She was given.
Sixty years accruing,
Her belongings spilled
Out of drawers and cupboards.
Her daughter's nightmare,
Charity workers' dream.
Sadly, she who all her life
Was fiercely possessive
And threw nothing out
Had no say in the end
When needy hands reached out
And charity was dispensed.

Eileen Monaghan

Innocent Daffodil

Why do you smile at me with your open yellow face
When you are destined for decapitation
To grace my kitchen vase?
Is it innocence?

Diana Guy

A Woman of Strength

I took my first faltering steps
Never to sit on mother's lap again
Another baby had taken my place
That giant hand brushed me aside
Her mind obsessed with other things
Growing up I kept my distance
Learned quickly how to please.
A child nurturing her mother
A child being the mother
Parish priest advised
"Put your children into an orphanage"
This tired grey-haired woman
Locked away her emotions
Raised her children
Against the angry tide.

Kathleen Brennan

The Decision

The waiting room was stuffy
Signs advertising counselling services
Broke the grey walls which
Reached down to the
Threadbare carpet
Where other feet had rested
As they waited their turn.

Had their owners also
Wrestled with guilty feelings
To come to the decision
Which had brought them to this place?
The grey evening light at London Airport
Mirrored the feelings in her heart.

She looked at her daughter
Brown eyes dwarfed the pale face
She reached over and gave her hand
A reassuring squeeze
Feeling closer to her now
They'd made the right choice.

It hadn't been an easy time
The rest of the family
Had to be considered
Another child would be too much
Her daughter's education had to come first
Things would work out.

The brown panelled door opened
The receptionist announced
"Next please"
As she walked through to the surgery
She looked back
Her daughter silently mouthed

"Good luck Mam"

Joan Cleere

Daughter to Mother

I know
this night you fear sleep
breath is such a blessing.

In silence we acknowledge death.

       Too great is your fear
       Too great is my despalr.

How I want to be your mother
Be you,   for you   now

Uncertain, I draw back from such an impulse
Resume my place in the order of things.

Daphne Hunt

Final Act

Time-Frame

This morning
You fed the robins
Surveyed the winter landscape
Left your footprints.

Evening found you
Beyond the Alps
While I trace your footsteps
In the Irish snow.

Rose Kelly

Extract from "Out of my Head"

Well, what can I say! It seemed a normal enough day, no different to any other. It was a Tuesday, and sure you know what Tuesdays are. If weeks came in graphs, the Tuesdays would just be creeping up, like a temperature rising. I got my husband up first. It wasn't difficult. He loves waking when he has work to go to. There was only about a week left though. He was taken on temporary because they got behind with the plastering. But his nerves were wrecked every time a man with a briefcase passed the site. You wonder is it worth it?

I roused the rest in the usual manner. Lies, deception, and a few clips round the ear. You know the sort of thing I mean. It's a quarter past when it's only a quarter to, then it's a quarter to when it's only a quarter past; and, of course, see this stick? Well, it's not for stirring the porridge with; That's the one that gets the best result. I make quite a bit of porridge. It's very good for them, and it's much cheaper. Mind you, penny wise and pound foolish my mother used to call me; or should it be the other way about? Anyway, a few stray hugs, a quick bless yourselves, a sort of rugby huddle in the hall to the tune of 'Angel of God my guardian dear,' and I don't need to tell you the relief that follows the closing of the front door.

Shaun was still moving around upstairs. His wee ACE job didn't start 'till half nine. It was only his third week and he was still newfangled. "Will these trousers be all right, Ma?" he shouted down, dangling a pair of slacks over the banisters. "Grand, son," I called back, the way you do without looking: The way your husband does when you ask him is your hair all right. I trusted him though. Shaun. He has good taste; not like me. I'll wear any old thing that comes to hand. It's all the same what you say to them anyway. They wear what they want to in the end. When he was ready for the off, he told me he was going to be a bit late home. "A project we're working on," he said, "A bit of overtime." "Right then," I said. "I'll hold your dinner till I see the whites of your eyes..." God!" The things you say.

I know he blessed himself for I saw him; even when they don't, I sometimes sprinkle a drop of holy water down the path after them; one of those habits you just can't break. But whether he said a prayer or not is another matter. He was past the stage of reciting the 'Angel of God' with me. I stood at the door and watched him to the end of the street. At the corner he turned and gave me a wave... I'll always be grateful for that at least.

Surely if I was going to feel anything was wrong, I should have felt it at that point? A pang of something with that last glimpse of him; a gut reaction of some sort. But I felt nothing. Where was my woman's intuition? Why did it not make me want to call him back? Beg him not to go out that day. Maybe I'm not a proper woman? So, all I did then was to look at the sky, decide not to risk any washing out, tap on Agnes's window and mouth, "Come in when you're ready," and I went back into the house to make the tea.

I suppose it's the laughter more than anything which stands out in my memory of that last morning of my other life; the one where I must have been completely happy, although I didn't know it at the time. Now I can't remember what it's like to wake up without this ache and longing inside me. My psychiatrist says it will pass, eventually; or at least get less. I'm not sure I'd like that.

Anyway, Agnes was in great form that day. She had been to a big bomb damage sale in Belfast, and got lots of stuff dead cheap. She showed me some of it.

There was a lovely wee suit for her Anne. She was making her Confirmation in a couple of weeks. 'Course they can wear anything now.' We laughed at the old fashioned white dresses we had to wear, and at the number of backs they'd been on before reaching us. Laughed too at the amount of money we collected on the day. Agnes recalled twenty-seven and six; I thought fifteen bob. It can run into hundreds now, confirmation money. They open bank accounts with it. We gave ours to our mothers, who were glad of it. I remarked to Agnes how you always seem to get bigger bargains in Belfast. "Well," she said, quick as a flash, "They get bigger bombs there don't they?" We both fell about at that, and I said, "God Agnes, you're terrible!" And we laughed some more. Then Agnes said, "Here, when's your Marie's confirmation? Maybe we can arrange something for that."

We had to hold our sides, and Agnes thought she'd wet herself. "The price you have to pay for having ten wanes," she groaned, "You can't even have a bloody good laugh!" The guilt I've felt since has been terrible... but what happened for all that wasn't my fault. Just remember that, my psychiatrist says. it was only idle talk.

After the children's lunch break the weather brightened up, and I was able to hang out the washing after all. I chatted to Angela from next door, the other side of me, and she was telling me how her son was getting on in England. "Great," she declared, "The money's good and he's staying with my sister." I remember I pitied her having a child so far away from home.

I think I started dinner early because George was laid off on account of a tip-off the firm got about an inspector on the snoop. Then my father phoned to say mother wasn't well. So I left George in charge of the kids and I went over to make the dinner for her and dad. It was my turn anyway to check on the two of them. We take turn about to do that, my sisters and me. Well, they were grand really. By the time I got there my mother's wee giddy spell had passed off, and she had father keeping an eye on the oven. We had a cosy chat with a cup of tea, and mother tried a jumper up against me that she was knitting. I admired it, and she said she was glad I liked it because it was for me anyway. I asked her what was father scowling at? "Don't talk to me," she said, "Hasn't he been banned from the club for a week. Him and old Micky had another barney last night. Now he doesn't know what to do with himself for the next while. And our May didn't help matters by telling him he could start a row in an empty house. "We both laughed at that. Then I was told about him across the street getting his compensation from work. Three thousand pounds! "Not much for a hop all the same," my mother said. "God bless the mark." I agreed; there were just some things you couldn't be compensated for.

I know I'm going to have trouble with this next bit, but this is the test isn't it? If I can get through these few minutes I'll be grand. I'll just take a good deep breath. And another. That's better. Let's see how far I can get now.

Well, my parents were settled at their dinner; I promised to send Emma over later with the Journal; I checked the kitchen clock against my watch; it was the usual ten minutes fast, my mother insisted on that always; it was five-thirty exactly. Just as I put my hand on the door-knob ready to go, we heard the explosion. It seemed the shake the house. The windows rattled. A plant fell off the sill. We all blessed ourselves, and the next thing I remember is me at the sink, with my mother holding my head while I vomited into the bowl. Then I collapsed. So, I was normal after all. My woman's intuition was intact. You have to be thankful for small mercies.

The journey home, we only lived round the corner from my parents, was a procession in itself. There was the priest and George holding me up. Then my father behind with a man who had come with the priest; turned out it was Shaun's boss. It seems he had let Shaun out for a few minutes to collect his girlfriend's birthday present from the jewellers, where he was having it engraved. Then, handy enough, wasn't he passing the van on his way back when it exploded. He was blown right through the bank window (not our bank) and was found in the new accounts section; well, most of him anyway. The whole street was crying. It's harder to know which travels faster, goods news or bad.

Myra Dryden

Another Good-bye

I tried to think of something to say
Something to soften your going away
But the words wouldn't come.

I stood there dry as a stick;
The inside of me all shrivelled up
with the drought of your leaving,
my droopy shoulders sagging,
wanting to cry,
wanting to give what you'd asked of me
and unable even to hug you.

For I knew if I hugged you
I'd say all the things
You wouldn't want me to say

So I leaned, with my shoulder pressed
to the frame of the door
and in a soft voice I mouthed
'Take care' – and 'Write me'
and watched you until you were gone

And when I was sure you were too far to hear,
the whole soft warm core of me
melted away at another good-bye.

Diana Guy

The Side Gate

The narrow gate
With the arched green hedge
Was locked for twenty-eight years
After his father's death.

On her wedding anniversary
His mother was waked
In her double bed.
Her sons now clipped the hedge
With pliers and hacksaw
Cut through rusty wire
Pulled and dragged
The gate swung open.

I watched this sacred ceremony
As they carried her coffin
Her last journey through her garden.
The end of tea being made from the aga
The end of teasing and betting on soccer matches
The end of home.

I closed the gate.

Anne Buckley

The Leave Taking

What were you thinking,
What was the matter
How could you go without a word
Did you give me a thought
As I sat waiting,
Wondering.

What was inside your head,
Did you hear voices
Did you have dark thoughts
Did you give me a thought
As I sat waiting,
Wondering.

Was the cold deep water more inviting
Than my warm ever loving arms
Did I not love you enough
Did you give me a thought
As I sat waiting,
Wondering,
Weeping.

Margo McCartney

Alzheimer's...

He 'took' her, went with her
Whatever...
He placed her
On the altar
Of sacrifice
Wearing his robes
Of guilt.

Dr High Priest said;
"She'll have to come in."

He sighed
As he folded
And put away
Carefully
In the drawer
Of forgetfulness
All the memories.

He could bring them to light later.
She never would.

Eileen Monaghan

Christmas Cards

"Jingle Bells, Jingle Bells"
Echoed through the shop
As I stopped to look at the
Christmas Cards
Traditional snow scenes
Stable with baby Jesus
Red-berried holly
Candles in windows
Loving greetings
To sons
Daughters
Fathers
Mothers...
I move on quickly
I won't be sending a card
To mother
This year

Joan Cleere

Death of a Child

How cruel of fate
To pluck so frail a bloom
And leave the gnarled old tree
With twisted arm and bended back
When death would set him free
From hours of pain.

Eileen Monaghan

The Last Journey

The ambulance stopped.
Two jovial uniformed men jumped out,
Massive in size, ruddy of complexion,
Oozing rude health, raw good humour and rough energy.

Together they reached the door,
Loud with bawdy banter, jovial jibe and light-hearted laughter

And then they saw their patient.

Suddenly transformed they were, into gentle giants.
Buttons straining on ill-fitting uniforms
They deftly lifted her.

A year past, she had been tall, strong and beautiful.

Now, prey to the wasting disease, she was fragile,
Frail and faded.

Gently they laid her on the stretcher,
Arranged the grey hospital blanket around her
With quiet words of comfort.

"The last journey," she whispered.

"Not at all, ma'am," they answered.
"You'll be home in a week, as well as ever you were."

And she smiled
And she knew
And they knew,
That it was the last journey

And all three went through the civility of pretending.

Sive Haughey

In Memory of Bobby

Stumbling slightly the boy
walks back from the altar

Red-rimmed eyes stare
uncomprehending

Small hands caress unyielding wood

No familiar arms to hug him

"I want my Daddy"

Slowly the grandfather
shuffles back to his seat

His gaze touches the
smooth shiny wood
his grief stark

No familiar arms to hold him

"I want my son"

Eileen Lynch

Final Act

Never was one for drama
can't handle it you see
it paralyses
thoughts
feelings
being;
all become absurd.

In the busy silence
of the ward
I wondered how they managed
to clean those lofty
old windows.

That night the clocks
went back,
as if it mattered.
'Only in silence does
sound have significance'
now who said that?

Perspiration spread into
the pillow and made
a halo round her head
hypnotising us.

My hands were wet and sticky
with her sweat
someone was sobbing
somewhere.

No trumpets
nor church bell
no favourite music
to mark her passing
just ... Bleep... bleep... bleep.

Helen Crimin

BIOGRAPHIES
BENNETTSBRIDGE WOMEN

Kathleen Brennan: Kathleen is a native of Kilkenny and has been writing for a few years. She found that the Bennettsbridge Writers sowed the seeds for writing and a love of her environment. In visiting Derry, meeting the women and sharing their stories, she has developed long-standing friendships.

Anne Buckley: Anne enjoys living within the old walls of Kilkenny surrounded by cathedral towers and grey steeples. Married to Paddy, with two children, Triona and Patrick. Anne's writing consists mainly of poetry and she has had work published in Syllabus, magazines, the local newspaper and has also read on radio. Anne's favourite memory of Derry was of walking with the Derry women to the Bogside and being told the story of 'Bloody Sunday'. She felt privileged as a woman from the South to be allowed into the private lives of her friends from Derry. These moments were precious and bonded Anne to the Derry women for all time.

Joan Cleere: Joan was born in Thomastown but has lived in Bennettsbridge since her marriage to Seamus. She has always been interested in writing and is local correspondent for the *Kilkenny People* newspaper since 1984. A member of the Bennettsbridge Writers since they were formed in 1989, Joan has had her work included in several Irish publications. She has also contributed to two previous books published by the group. Joan likes to record memories of her childhood and growing up in Thomastown. Her special memory of Derry is of visiting the Bogside and the Museum and the friendships formed through the Derry connection.

Helen Crimin: Helen is an Irish woman born and raised in Scotland who has now come home. Writing is a new and wonderful experience for her. Since she started writing about five years ago she has had her work published in three anthologies. She is, therefore, truly delighted with her achievements to date. Helen's Derry experience was, for her, the "icing on the cake."

Daphne Hunt: Daphne was born in Dublin in 1945. She has lived in Kilkenny for the past twenty-five years between Mount Brandon and the River Nore. Daphne has been a member of the Bennettsbridge Writers since its inception celebrating motherhood, daughterhood, sharing the joys and tears of life with extraordinary women. She has had poems published in several anthologies of women's poetry. Her visits North meant overcoming fear, passing armoured cars, checkpoints; trying not to appear conspicuous, until friendship replaced fear and she was no longer awkward.

Mary-Margaret Kelly: Mary-Margaret is a native of Thomastown, County Kilkenny. She is a student and won the Sean Dunne Young Writers Award 1997 in Waterford and has been commissioned to write for Waterford Review 1998.

Rose Kelly: Rose is a primary school teacher. She has previously been published in two group publications, also in the *Waterford Review* and *Cuirt, Poets Platform*. Rose likes to write about things that touch the soul. Rose enjoys the new dimension that the Northern contact has brought to her life.

Phil Kennedy: Phil lives in Bennettsbridge and is a member of the Bennettsbridge Writers Group since it was first formed in 1989. She has had some of her poems read on local radio and RTE and has also had a poem published in an anthology of women's poetry produced by The Works, Wexford. They told Phil that Derry was a beautiful City with friendly people and she says "They weren't wrong!"

Elma Khareghani: Elma lives in Kilkenny. She loves writing poetry, when inspired, mainly about the environment. She has recently taken up painting as a hobby. She was a founder member of the Bennettsbridge Writers. She is as old as she feels, today about twenty-five, tomorrow maybe fifty. Elma admires the 'ordinary' people of Northern Ireland who work hard to bring about a reconciliating and fundamental change in their communities. She fell in love with Derry and its people and feels that her grandchildren will live and grow up in an atmosphere of peace and harmony on this Isle of Ireland.

Daphne Kirkpatrick: Daphne lived in Ireland for about three years having pursued a lengthy teaching career in Scotland. A Channel Islander by birth she identifies strongly with Irish life since it is reminiscent of her childhood in Jersey. She has written poetry on and off since she was six and has had work published and broadcast in Scotland. Daphne now lives in Cornwall.

Eileen Lynch: Eileen is originally from Carrick-on-Suir but now lives in Kilkenny with her two children, Margaret and Neil. She has been a member of the Bennettsbridge group for the past four years. Eileen has great admiration for the Derry women that she met during the exchanges; they manage to rear a family and cope with the stresses of living in the North of Ireland and are still ready to have the "bit of craic" when they visit the South.

Anne McLoughlin: Anne is originally from Scotland and has lived in Ireland for twenty-one years. Married with three grown children Ann has been involved in adult education for many years, particularly working with women's groups in the area of self-development, assertiveness and stress management. She has also worked as a facilitator with Co-operation North with cross border exchange groups including the Bennettsbridge/Derry women writers. Being an 'honorary member' of the group has been a great privilege and being involved in the exchanges has given her insights into the role of women in Derry.

Janie Richardson: Janie was born in England but has lived in Ireland for the past twenty-six years and is as 'Irish' as one can get! Her two sons, Christian and Revere, were born in Ireland. In the past Janie wrote for newspapers and magazines but now writes for the love of writing and has published her poetry in the group publications *Daughters of the Wind* and *Tangerine Skies*. She has read her poetry on radio and has given workshops in creative writing. The Derry 'experience' has been more than just about forming enduring friendships, it has been an exchange of attitudes, a breaking down of barriers and prejudices, a journey through history, a voyage of discovery and the precursor to lasting memories.

DERRY WOMEN

Ina Cantrell: Ina was born in Ireland but most of her life has lived in the USA where she was a teacher, writer, broadcaster and storyteller. Ina has now returned to Ireland and continues writing and sharing true ghost stories under the name of 'The Ghost Host' and doing cross-community projects with both children and adults. Her memorable experiences shared with the women from Kilkenny has served to remind her that there are more similarities than differences, and it is her fervent hope that the bridges built will be bridges to peace and understanding.

Myra Dryden: Epitome of the aphorism 'You can take the girl out of Derry, but you can't take Derry out of the girl'. Fiercely interested in English/Anglo-Irish literature, Myra is influenced by Sterne and Beckett, though sadly, she says, unable to emulate either yet! She is determined to keep trying though.

Diana Guy: Diana is Canadian and emigrated to Northern Ireland in 1964. She has lived in many areas of the province and finally settled in Bushmills 11 years ago. She writes mainly for pleasure and her work has a strong Canadian flavour. She has been published in several anthologies and in the local paper. Her visits to Bennettsbridge have become a celebration of friendship. She feels that the richness of shared experience and the strength that has come from our togetherness as women has helped her to realise the power we possess as individuals to create change within our communities.

Sive Haughey: Sive spent her childhood in Belleek, County Fermanagh. She was educated at Queen's University, Belfast and St Mary's Training College, Belfast. Sive taught French and Irish in Belfast, Cookstown and finally in Derry. She has had short stories and poems published in several anthologies and periodicals and her novel is due for publication in Autumn 1997. Sive loves to read, walk and nurture her garden.

Eilis Heaney: Eilis was born into an old Derry family, the youngest of thirteen. She became the mother of thirteen children. Sadly her youngest son was killed in 1978 by the British Army. She was widowed in 1985. Eilis began writing in 1989 and has had poetry and prose in several publications such as *Our Say, Awakenings, Jukin Back* and Fingerpost Magazine. Eilis has happy memories of her meetings with the Kilkenny women on their visits to Derry. They were all so warm and friendly and when she talked to some of them of the death of her son Dennis, their genuine interest and understanding was indeed very heart warming and consoling. Regrettably Eilis was unable to travel to Kilkenny because of her health at the time of our group's visits there. She looks forward to meeting up with them again, hopefully at the launch of the book.

Chris Head: Chris promotes community based adult education programmes for the Northern Ireland WEA. She lives as creatively as possible through writing, painting, drawing, making pottery, print making and any other methods she needs to challenge, comment and celebrate the experience of being human. "What I have experienced and observed through participating in the Co-operation North exchange programme are individuals who have flourished and contributed their talents, skills and personalities to the group process in a positive way. What we share is the will to share and that is a seriously wonderful thing."

Margo McCartney: Margo began writing five years ago. Her work has been published in various magazines and anthologies. She is involved with cross-community and cross border women's writing groups. "After our first meeting with the Kilkenny women I was surprised to find we had so much with people from a different culture and environment, so much so, that as well as being women writers together solid friendships have been formed that will last longer than we even could have imagined. I feel honoured and proud to have been a part of this exciting project."

Eileen Monaghan: Eileen was born and has lived in Derry all her life. She has been writing poetry since her school days; it seemed to come naturally to her. She left school at fourteen years of age and has been involved in writing groups organised by the WEA and the Verbal Arts Centre. Eileen has given poetry readings and has had short stories, articles and poetry published. "We had great weekends with the Kilkenny writers. It was as if we had known them all our lives."

Linda Morgan: Linda was born in Derry into a family of six boys and has one younger sister. She has lived happily in Derry since she was married in 1988. Linda attended her first creative writing class in the Women's Centre, Pump Street, in 1992 and since then has been involved in a number of projects and is a tutor in creative writing for the WEA. Linda is also a member of the 'Maiden City Writers', a newly formed cross community writing group, and is currently studying for a degree in English Literature with the Open University.

Perceptions – Cultures in Conflict
Compiled by Adrian Kerr

Seeing is Believing – Murals in Derry
Oona Woods

The Road to Bloody Sunday
Dr Raymond McClean

No Go – A Photographic
Record of Free Derry
Barney McMonagle

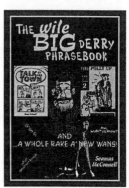

The Wile Big Derry
Phrasebook
Seamus McConnell

Parade of Phantoms II
Peter Mc Cartney